Beneath My Ribs

Verses for the days that split me open

Lexie Brewer

BookLeaf
Publishing

India | USA | UK

Made with ❤ on the BookLeaf Publishing Platform
www.bookleafpub.in
www.bookleafpub.com

Dedication

To Sandy Brown,
who never asked me to be anyone but myself.
You once said,
"I may not have been the best teacher,
but I helped my students find Jesus
and I loved them where they were."
You did exactly that—
and it was your way of being,
not just your words,
that left an imprint on my life.

To Gene McKelroy,
who saw me clearly,
and offered me the quiet gift
of space to be who I already was—
with gentle guidance
and true kindness.

To my Mom and Kristal,
for believing in me
in every season,
and for loving me
without conditions.

And to my son, Harlan—
who I love more than anything
in this world.
My only hope
is to make you
so, so proud.

You have all shaped
the voice on these pages.
This book belongs to you, too.

Preface

This book holds small fragments of my heart—snippets
of thought gathered from the chaos of living and loving
and losing and trying again.

Most of these words began as messy, sprawling brain
dumps, scribbled in the quiet hours when the world felt
too heavy, or too loud, or sometimes heartbreakingly
silent. Over the last two years, writing became the one
thing I could reach for when everything else felt too far
away. It cost me nothing but time and truth—and gave
me, in return, a place to lay down the weight I carried
while hurting, healing, mothering, and existing in all the
spaces between.

I know how lucky I am to have words as a refuge, but
even the most beautiful words feel hollow if kept hidden.
So I'm sharing these pieces not because I think they're
perfect—but because I believe stories and feelings are
meant to be witnessed.

My biggest reason for letting these pages breathe beyond
my own hands is my son, Harlan. I want him to know
that dreams don't have an expiration date. That you're
never too young, too old, too broken, too busy—or "too

anything"—to try. To begin again. To chase the best, truest version of yourself, even if your hands are trembling as you reach.

If these poems do nothing else, I hope they remind him— and maybe you—that it's brave to speak your heart out loud. And that it's never too late to turn the mess inside you into something that glows.

Welcome to my heart on paper.

— Lex

Acknowledgements

To the ones who, time and again, looked me in the eyes and said, "You should write a book."

Your words were more than casual encouragement—they were gentle pushes forward on days I wanted to quit, lifelines tossed into the dark when doubt felt too heavy to bear. Your belief has been the quiet fuel behind every line, every page, every trembling moment I chose to keep writing instead of giving up.

To Ravyn, Lauren, Taylor , Baile, and Garrett—thank you for believing in me in all things. For talking me off countless ledges, for reminding me I'm never foolish for feeling too much or for wanting to turn my chaos into poetry. You have each been my safe place, my laughter on hard days, and my proof that love can look like friendship holding the pieces of me steady.

I love you more than words will ever stretch to say—but beyond love, I am deeply grateful. Grateful to have the village that is you, standing beside me in every chapter of this wild, messy, beautiful life.

This book carries my name on its cover, but it carries

pieces of all of you inside it.

Thank you, from the bottom of my heart.

— Lex, Sister, Biiiiiiitch, Best Friend, Babe

1. Where The Enemy Lurks

He doesn't come with horns.
Not for women like me.
Not for mothers who bear both the weight and the
wonder,
who hold it all together with trembling hands and tired
hearts.

He waits until the house is quiet—
until the toys are scattered,
the baby's finally asleep,
and I'm left with nothing but my own breath and my
own thoughts.

Then he whispers:
"You're not doing enough."
"They'll be better off without your mess."
"You shouldn't be this angry."
"This lonely."
"This tired."

He doesn't roar.
He drips—
Guilt in my coffee.
Fear in my laundry.

Shame in the mirror.
Comparison in my scroll.

He twists my independence into isolation.
My strength into walls.
My softness into weakness.

But what he forgets is this:
I've survived things he wouldn't dare walk through.
And I show up anyway.
For my child.
For myself.
For the story I'm still writing.

So if he's after me—
Good.
It means I'm a threat.

2. Seven Rounds

I remember the journey.
The quiet war of hope and disappointment.
The calendar marked in red—
days counted forward,
then counted down.
Temperature charts like battleground maps.
Pee sticks lined up like soldiers.
Apps buzzing with reminders.
Meds stacked like fragile prayers.

I remember leaving for work late,
just so my husband could hold me—
could try, one more time,
before his night shift swallowed him whole.
I remember the clock.
The science.
The 5 years and 7 rounds.
The ache that settled in my bones like winter.
The way disappointment made a home in me,
but hope never fully moved out.

And still,
if I had to walk through that fire again—
month after month,

test after test,
cry after silent cry—
I would.
Without hesitation.
Because the child I hold now...
he was worth every unanswered prayer
that led me to the right one.

He came without help.
No plan. No prediction.
No perfect timing—
except God's.

And I see now—
it was never a denial.
Only a delay.
A sacred pause,
for a purpose I couldn't yet understand.

If I could go back,
I'd whisper to that weary woman:
"Hold on.
The wait is not wasted.
There is a child meant just for you—
and he's coming,
not when you expect,
but exactly when you're ready

to love him the way only you can."

God was never late.
He was planting something deeper.
A purpose only *he* could carry.
A soul with timing all his own.

And I would wait forever again
just to meet him
exactly how he came.

3. The Boys In Mud

It stormed last night.
The kind that shakes windows and rinses the world
clean.
And now, under a hot June sun,
my boys are out there—shirtless, barefoot, wild—
splashing through leftover puddles like they were made
just for them.

They've done it all this morning.
Caught worms with gentle hands, chased frogs across
the yard,
and screamed their discoveries to the sky
like the universe should know: *We are alive. We are loud.*
We are here.

And I—
well, I'm sitting with coffee in hand,
legs tucked beneath me,
just watching.

I should probably stop them from flinging mud at each
other,
or at least pretend I care about the laundry.
But I don't.

Not right now.

Because in this moment—
as they stomp and laugh and fall and rise again,
as the dog barks and the cicadas buzz in the distance—
I am overwhelmed with thankfulness.

Not just the kind you post about.
The kind that lives in the throat,
the chest,
the soft ache behind the eyes.

I love them so easily.
So wholly.
Even when they're loud. Even when they're muddy.
Maybe especially then.

Because this is what childhood should look like—
bare feet, full hearts, and the kind of joy
you can hear from down the street.

And this is what motherhood feels like—
being the quiet observer
of everything sacred.

6. Where The Celebration Ended

I remember.

It was your first birthday.
Balloons still hanging low from the ceiling,
frosting smudged into your curls,
and a heaviness in my chest that didn't belong to the
moment.
Somewhere deep in my bones—I just knew.

I waited until the guests left.
Until the kitchen was quiet.
And then I took the test.
Clear blue. Pregnant.
And I cried—harder than I knew I could.

How could I ever love another child the way I loved you?
How did we only get one uninterrupted year?
One year where my arms were just yours?
What if you had to share me—would you feel less
chosen?
Would you think my heart had less room?
That your place in it could be edged out?

I didn't even tell your dad.
I couldn't.
I dreaded what it meant—pregnancy again, so soon.
I was still climbing out of the hollow cave of postpartum.
Still bleeding in ways no one could see.
And now more chaos. More ache.
More pretending everything was fine.

Your dad and I—we weren't even sure we liked each
other anymore.
Just coexisting with a shared love for you and little else.
And now this.

But I wanted to want it.
So I paid for pictures.
Got you a "Big Brother" shirt.
Planned the surprise.
Let myself imagine the joy I wasn't sure I could feel.

Then came the first appointment.
No heartbeat.
The room got quieter than quiet.
And then the bleeding.
And then the second ultrasound that confirmed what my
body already knew.

Miscarriage.

And just like that—
Gone.

Back to "normal."
Except nothing was.
Except now I was grieving two versions of myself—
the one who knew joy,
and the one who had to carry the loss in silence.
Back to singing songs, packing snacks, playing peek-a-
boo—
while bleeding through it all.

No one could see the hollowed-out parts.
No one noticed the ghost I carried.
But I remember.
And I always will.

Because that week, I learned something brutal:
you can be endlessly thankful
and completely gutted
at the very same time.

4. Where The Darkness Ends

"Safe adults don't keep secrets,"
I say for the third time today.
His little brow furrows,
his imagination spinning stories—
What if it's a birthday surprise? What if it's about a toy?
The innocence in his voice
is almost too much to bear.

I answer every question,
patiently, carefully—
but with a fire he doesn't yet understand.
Because he doesn't know why.
Not really.
But I do.

I know the shadows that wear smiles.
The danger that sometimes looks like trust.
I know what it means
to carry secrets that were never mine to hold—
heavy, confusing,
spoken in whispers and shame.

So I say it again.

And again.
Until it roots itself in him.

We don't keep secrets for adults.
Not the silly ones. Not the scary ones.
If it needs to be hidden,
it needs to be spoken.

Because I am his light.
His line of defense.
And I will not let the darkness slip past me
dressed as innocence.

So he plays with Legos,
asks about dragons,
tells me he's pretending to be a superhero.

And I nod,
because he already is.
He just doesn't know
that being able to tell the truth
might be his first superpower.

6. Harlan

My son is magic and starlight—
a spark in the darkness,
a glow I never knew my heart could hold.

He is tiny hands
wrapped around my fingers,
melting every hardened piece of me
with the simplest touch.

He has the bluest eyes—
oceans I could drown in,
reflecting wonder, mischief,
and a thousand silent questions
about the world.

His laugh is the sweetest sound
I have ever known—
like bells, like summer wind,
like the universe pausing
just to listen.

He is filled to the brim
with piggy pie sugars,
a sweetness that sticks

to the edges of my days,
making everything softer,
gentler,
worthwhile.

And inside his small chest
beats the kindest heart—
a heart that forgives easily,
loves without question,
and teaches me,
again and again,
what it means to be
truly good.

My son is proof
that magic exists,
that starlight finds its way
even into the darkest nights.

He is my reason,
my hope,
and every quiet prayer
I've ever whispered
into the hush
before dawn.

7. Half a Home, Whole a Heart

Funny how life can split
right down the middle—
the before and the after.

How one day
you're picking out china patterns,
saying forever,
believing love alone
will keep the walls from crumbling.

And then one day
you're learning how to pack
tiny backpacks
for weekends away,
smiling so your kids
don't see the cracks
in your voice.

Nobody tells you
how hard it is
to keep laughing
when your world
is coming apart

in courtrooms
and calendars.

Nobody warns you
that bedtime stories
sometimes have to cover
the echo of your own loneliness,
or that silence
can roar so loud
it rattles every window
in the house.

Nobody expects
the paperwork,
the negotiations,
the holidays split
like a wishbone,
or the guilt that digs in
every time your kids
walk out the door
with someone else.

But here we are—
still figuring it out,
still putting one foot
in front of the other,
still pasting on smiles

like fresh paint
over peeling walls.

Because if there's one thing
I know now—

It's that we'd do anything
to help our kids
keep believing
in happy endings,

even when ours
looks nothing like
the one
we dreamed.

8. Leave The Second Time

They say leave the first time.
The first time he raises his voice,
the first time his hand lands too close to fear,
the first time he calls you something ugly and means it.

And they're right—
God, they're right.
But they don't understand what it feels like to still love someone
who's already started breaking you.

They don't know how soft hope can sound
when it whispers, "Maybe it was just once."
Maybe he was tired.
Maybe I pushed too hard.
Maybe if I love him better, he'll love me gently again.

You convince yourself that love can fix it.
That grace can teach him tenderness.
That your silence is strength.

You tuck the hurt under your tongue
and call it forgiveness.
You trace the bruises in your heart

and call them proof that you tried.

But listen to me—
leave the second time.

Leave when his apologies start to sound rehearsed.
Leave when your body flinches before your mind does.
Leave when you realize you've started waiting for peace
in a place that keeps handing you pain.

Leave even if you still love him.
Even if he's crying.
Even if your knees shake when you pack your things.

Leave before you start confusing survival for devotion.
Before you start calling your own slow death
commitment.

Because the truth is—
you don't owe anyone the version of you that keeps
bleeding to make them whole.

So if you couldn't leave the first time—
if love blinded you, if fear silenced you—
leave the second time.
Hell, even the third.

Just don't stay long enough to forget that you deserve to be safe.

To be soft.

To be loved and not repaired.

9. Her

Here's to the friends
who make life, life.

The childhood friend
who knew your middle name,
your favorite color,
who swapped bras and lip gloss
and secrets whispered in the dark.
Who was there for proms,
first heartbreaks,
and summer nights
that smelled like freedom
and cheap perfume.

The friend who showed up later—
maybe in a college dorm,
or a smoky bar,
who held your hair back
after cheap vodka,
who danced beside you
like you owned the night,
who stayed up talking
until sunrise felt holy.

The friend who arrived
when the ground split open—
who held you close
while your marriage fell apart,
who listened without flinching
as you confessed
you didn't know who you were anymore.
Who helped you believe
that starting over
doesn't mean starting empty.

The mom friends—
who know the language
of nap schedules and meltdowns,
who drop off coffee
on the mornings
you're drowning,
who love your kids
like their own.

Here's to all of them—
the old,
the new,
the fleeting,
the forever—

Each one a thread

woven into the fabric
of who we are.

Life wouldn't be life
without them.

10. Jeri

ome people move through the world
carrying a quiet kind of brilliance—
a shimmer you can't name,
but feel in your bones.

She was like that.
Though I met her later in life,
it was clear she stood apart
from the edges of everyone else—
as if she carried hidden colors
where the family tended to stay
in shades of safe and same.

She was a watchmaker,
spinning tiny gears
into perfect rhythm.
She'd tell me stories
about her work,
her fingers shaping invisible pieces
in the air as she spoke—
and it felt like she was letting me in
on some small, wondrous secret.

She'd tell me funny stories, too—

about life, about people,
about moments that made her laugh
like she'd known me forever.

And when motherhood
swallowed me whole
and I felt unseen
in the blur of days,
she found me.
A message. A check-in.
Proof that I mattered.
Proof that someone remembered
who I was.

She was a rainbow,
woven from brilliance and softness,
standing unapologetically apart—
and somehow,
that made her feel closer to me.

Now, I like to think
she's finally up close
to the rainbow she always was—
all those colors
gathered around her,
welcoming her home.

And though the world feels dimmer
without her here,
her light remains—
in the stories she shared,
in the moments she saw me,
in the quiet shimmer
she left behind.

11. Our Monster

Addiction.

It's a thief that creeps in slow,
disguised at first as something manageable—
a bad habit,
a rough patch,
a phase.

And before you know it,
it's gutted the house
you once believed could hold
a happy, traditional family.

The kind with laughter over dinner,
inside jokes,
quiet nights under soft lamp light,
holidays untouched by chaos.

Instead—
there's screaming behind doors,
lies stacked like dishes in the sink,
the sour smell of secrets
hanging in the curtains.

It's wild,
how hope clings on
even as you watch them disappear—
believing you can fix them,
love them enough to make them choose
you
over the bottle,
the pill,
the powder,
the thrill.

Believing one day they'll become
the parent you needed,
the partner you prayed for,
the steady hand instead of
the trembling one.

But the truth?

Addiction doesn't care
about family photos on the mantle,
tiny hands reaching up for comfort,
promises made in trembling voices.

It burns through everything—
birthdays, anniversaries,
Christmas mornings—

until all that's left
is the rubble of what might have been.

And the rest of us?

We're left wandering the ruins,
trying to stitch together
a version of family
that doesn't feel like a lie.

Haunted by echoes of laughter
that belonged to a life
we'll never get back.

Because sometimes love
isn't enough to save them.

And sometimes the bravest thing
is admitting
you can't keep drowning
trying to pull someone
to the surface.

12. Mom

An ode to the mothers
who were mean as rattlesnakes
when life cornered them,
whose love could cut like glass
and still somehow
hold the whole world together.

Mothers who didn't always
have it together—
who sometimes didn't have it at all.

Mothers who packed up homes
in the hush of midnight,
who kept chasing the promise
that somewhere else
might be softer,
gentler,
kinder.

Mothers whose tired hands
punched time clocks,
whose eyes grew glassy
with worry and weariness,
who came home

carrying storms in their chest.

Mothers whose tempers flared
like thunderheads,
whose laughter could vanish
just as quickly,
leaving silence
thick as humidity
before a summer downpour.

Mothers who taught us
to listen for the weather
in the pattern of their footsteps—
soft or sharp,
fast or dragging—
each echo a warning
or an invitation.

But even then—
we knew they loved us.
Fiercely.
Unevenly.
In the best way
they knew how.

And now,
we daughters stand

with children of our own
pressed against our beating hearts,
and we feel the old ache
rise up like a storm cloud,
the vow blooming quietly:

I will do it differently.

Not because we don't love
the women who raised us—
but because we do.

Because we know now
what it costs
to hold a family together
while your own seams split open.

Motherhood, we've learned,
is choosing softness
where there once was steel,
building bridges
where there once were walls,
and teaching tiny hearts
they never have to earn
a place in ours.

So here's to the mothers

who did the best they could
with weathered hands
and weary hearts—

and to the daughters
who became mothers,
determined to love
like gentle rain
instead of thunder.

13. Daisy Doodle

Four paws,
a wagging tail,
ears like soft flannel,
and eyes that have seen every version of me—
the good, the wrecked, the trying.

She's been there
when I was too heartbroken to speak.
When the house echoed from emptiness or newborn
cries.
When I needed to be held
but didn't want to ask.

She's seen it all—
the slammed doors,
the whispered prayers,
the quiet celebrations no one else noticed.
She never flinched.
She just stayed.

She's been climbed on by sticky toddler hands,
used as a pillow for nap time,
and pulled into blanket forts like royalty.
And she's never once pulled away.

Only leaned in.

She's more than a dog.
She's a witness.
To the undoing.
To the becoming.

And if I could buy her forever
with every last thing I own—
I would.

Because in a world that never stopped shifting,
she was the one thing
that never let go.

And loving her
might be the purest,
most faithful thing
I've ever done.

14. The Sacred Unseen

It's worth creating
even if no one claps.
Even if the likes don't pour in
and the algorithm looks the other way.

It's worth writing
what shakes inside your chest,
painting the ache,
capturing the softness,
even if no one sees it but you.

Not everything sacred
needs to be shared.
Not every offering
needs a stage.

You don't need an audience
to make something real.
You just need the guts
to make it anyway.

15. Whiskey Doesn't Text Back

Most nights I sip something civilized.
An espresso martini because I like pretending I have taste.
A stout if I want to feel grounded.
A porter when I'm lying to myself about being chill.

But tonight?

I want a cigarette.
A cowboy killer.
Marlboro Red, no apologies.
I want it to light up like a warning sign,
fill my lungs with something that says *I don't care anymore—*
even if I do. Especially because I do.

And I want a whiskey. Neat.
Not something dressed in citrus or poured over ice cubes shaped like diamonds.
I want the kind that burns on the way down
and reminds you you're still here
even when you wish you weren't.

I'm not going to do it.
Because I've got "self-control" now.
Because I quit years ago.
Because I'm someone's mother.
Because healing looks good on paper,
but god, it's boring at night.

And no, the whiskey doesn't miss me.
It's not wondering where I've been.
It's not aching in my absence.
It moved on without flinching—
like everyone else eventually does.

Still—
tonight I want to come undone.
Not in a dramatic, throw-things kind of way.
Just quietly.
The kind of unraveling that happens in silence,
when nobody's watching,
and everything finally spills.

16. Dear Younger Me

Go on the trip.
Pack light, and take the long way.

Snorkel when you get the chance—
let salt water teach you there's a whole world beneath
the surface.

Take the job. Or don't.
Both roads lead somewhere worth discovering.

That boy? He always circles back,
but know you won't always be there waiting.

Those friends you cried over really did suck.
The few who didn't?
They're the scaffolding of your entire life.

That cheap vodka won't hit the same at thirty—
but the hangovers will hit harder,
linger longer,
make you swear off shots (until you don't).

Your mother knows more than you think.
Listen closely. One day, her voice

will echo in yours.

Don't take your dog for granted.
She won't always be there,
waiting at the door with a tail that forgives everything.

And karma always collects—
so whatever you are,
be a good one.

Shake hands firmly.
Look people in the eye when you speak.
Speak truth, even when it trembles.

But above all:

Travel.
Jump out of planes.
Eat the strange food.
Climb the rock wall.
Walk the spine of the mountain.
Drink the drink.
Snorkel when you get the chance.
Talk to strangers who might become friends.

Live.
Live as deeply as you dare.

Trust me: it all works out in the end.

This is what I'd tell you,
and then I'd wrap you in my arms
and thank you—for your bravery,
for your softness,
for becoming me.

17. Save Ya a Seat

My cousin always says,
"I'd rather build a bigger table
than tell people they can't join."

And those words live in me
like a quiet promise—
a soft rebellion against a world
that loves gates and velvet ropes,
guest lists and locked doors.

Because I know how it feels
to stand outside the glow of a room,
heart pounding,
wondering what makes me unworthy
of a seat inside.

I remember
the silence after a joke falls flat,
the polite nods,
the way people look past you
like you're invisible.

And so I swore:
not in my house.

Not at my table.

I'll keep adding chairs,
stretching the wood,
laying mismatched plates
because everyone deserves
a place to set down
their burdens,
their stories,
their weary hands.

I want laughter so loud
it shakes the windows,
voices layered in a chorus
of accents, histories, hopes.

I want the ones
who've been told they're too much,
too different,
too complicated—
to come and find themselves
welcomed, wanted,
exactly as they are.

Because the world builds walls.
But I?

I'll keep building
a bigger table.

18. Karmas Collection

I finally found the love of my life.
The kind that softens the sharpest edges,
that feels like warm hands on cold skin—
steady, sure, safe.

But I owed Karma one.
And she never forgets.

Maybe it was a debt from years ago—
from hearts I held carelessly,
or lessons I refused to learn
until they were carved into me.

So just as I exhaled—
just as I started to believe
that maybe love could stay—
the ground gave out.

Not in a blaze,
but in quiet undoings.
Little shifts. Little losses.
Until what felt like forever
turned into *almost*.

I loved him.
God, I still might.
But sometimes the universe doesn't ask if you're ready.
Sometimes it just takes what was borrowed.

And maybe he was never mine to keep—
just mine to meet.
To soften something in me,
even as he left something behind.

Karma always collects.
But she taught me what love could be.
And maybe... that's worth the cost.

19. JUST GIVE A FUCK

I didn't want much.
Just for him to give a fuck.

Not the half-hearted, "sorry you feel that way" kind.
Not the performative check-in that comes with a sigh
and a clock behind his eyes.
I wanted the real kind—
the "I see you, I hear you, I choose you" kind.

I got tired of being a broken record in a room with the
volume down.
Same conversation.
Different day.
Same ache.
Different silence.

And God, I tried.
I begged—quietly at first, then louder,
then with eyes that didn't sparkle anymore.
Just give a fuck.
Just try.

I told myself I'm not hard to love.
I still believe that.

Or maybe I'm wrong?
Maybe I'm too much and too loud and too all-at-once.

But if I had to bet on it—
I'd bet that loving me is easier than undoing all the
reckless promises
we made in the name of a forever that didn't show up.

Regret's cheap ink.
But I?
I am not.

20. The Comedian

I'm furious.
Sad.
Lava-in-my-bones, scream-into-a-pillow, punch-a-hole-in-drywall kind of unwell.
(But with good aim, and decent upper body strength, so
—watch your Sheetrock.)

I've survived wars no one wrote home about.
Not the kind with tanks and tactics,
but the kind where love is the battlefield
and I'm out here dodging criticism like sniper fire
while waving a little white flag made out of sarcasm and
"I'm fines."

And honestly?
I should get a purple heart for staying in relationships
where I was the only one bleeding.

But I show up.
Mascara on.
Jokes loaded.
Smile so convincing it could win an Oscar—or at least a
pity latte from the barista.
And I play the role.

I'm the comic relief in my own Greek tragedy.
Tripping over trauma with a punchline in hand.

Because if I don't laugh,
I might start crying and just...
never stop.

So yeah, I'm unraveling.
Like a cheap sweater on clearance.
But at least I'm funny.

21. Lover

I found him.

Safety, somehow,
in the space where I come undone—
where my edges soften,
and my truths spill out
unafraid.

A love I pray
isn't a brief flicker,
but a steady flame—
an anchor,
an echo of forever
pressed close against my chest.

He has kaleidoscope eyes—
colors shifting with every glance,
sometimes playful,
sometimes dark with wanting,
always looking at me
like I'm something rare
he can't believe he's holding.

Golden skin that glows

like the hush before sunrise,
warmth radiating into mine,
even in the quiet brush
of his fingertips across my wrist—
a touch so gentle
it leaves fire in its wake.

Strong hands,
soft with me—
confident enough
to guide me closer,
tender enough
to make me feel cherished
even when the air between us
grows electric.

With him,
even the familiar streets
of our hometown
feel like adventure—
laughing in hidden corners,
sharing secrets over midnight coffee,
finding places to steal a kiss
that tastes like something
worth remembering.

And the way he speaks—

like each word is chosen
to soothe me,
to tease me,
to tell me I'm safe,
and wanted,
and his.

I found him.
And in his arms,
love feels not only possible,
but inevitable—
something beautiful,
wild,
and entirely mine.